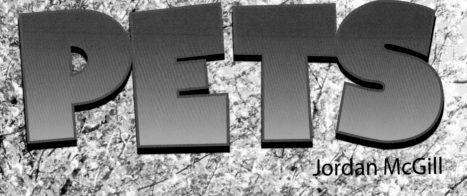

PETS

Jordan McGill

www.av2books.com

Step 1

Go to **www.av2books.com**

Step 2

Enter this unique code

XQNMFZFN5

Step 3

Explore your interactive eBook!

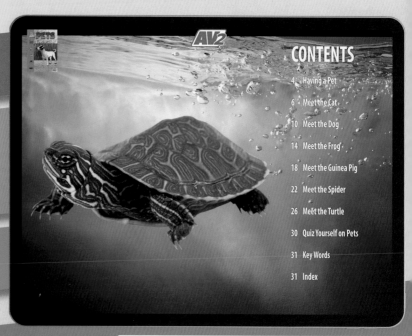

AV2 is optimized for use on any device

Your interactive eBook comes with...

Contents
Browse a live contents page to easily navigate through resources

Audio
Listen to sections of the book read aloud

Videos
Watch informative video clips

Weblinks
Gain additional information for research

Try This!
Complete activities and hands-on experiments

Key Words
Study vocabulary, and complete a matching word activity

Quizzes
Test your knowledge

Slideshows
View images and captions

... and much, much more!

PETS

CONTENTS

HAVING A PET

Caring for a pet is a big responsibility. Some pets, such as dogs and cats, are large and take much care. Others, such as frogs and spiders, are small and easy to care for. Whatever pet someone chooses to keep, care must be taken because pets rely on their owners to survive.

All pets require food and a home. Some pets need a little more. Small animals, such as frogs, guinea pigs, and spiders to name a few, are quite small and need little exercise. They mostly live in small **habitats**. Larger animals, such as dogs and cats, need more care and attention. Cats need room to roam, and dogs need to be taken on daily walks.

WHY DRAW?

triangles

Drawing pets is a great way to learn more about the animals and what features make them unique. This can help you determine which pet would suit you best and why. It can also help you decide whether the features of the pets make them a good fit for your home.

Look around you. The world is made of shapes and lines. By combining simple shapes and lines, anything can be drawn. A horse's ears are just triangles with a few details added. A rabbit's eye can be a circle. Almost anything, no matter how complicated, can be broken down into simple shapes.

circle →

What shapes do you see in this goldfish?

Meet the
CAT

Whether an alley cat or a majestic lion, all cats have certain features in common. Most cats have fur on their bodies to keep them warm. Cats are fast, agile, strong, and smart. Their senses are keen and sensitive. These characteristics help make the cat a great hunter. Even pet cats hunt mice and birds.

Eyes
Cats can see in the dark about six times better than humans. A cat's **pupils** grow very large and round in low light. This allows more light to enter. In bright light, a cat's pupils become narrow slits.

Nose
Even before they can see, kittens use their sharp sense of smell to guide them. A cat's nose can tell it what was in a room before it enters.

Paws
Domestic cats can run about 30 miles (48 kilometers) per hour. Cats also have sharp **retractable claws**. The bottoms of their paws are protected by tough pads.

Ears
Cats have very good hearing. They can move their ears to locate sounds. Each ear can be moved **independently** and can turn 180 degrees.

Tail
A cat's tail is an extension of its backbone. Cats use their tail for balance and to show their mood.

Back Legs
Very strong back legs help cats jump onto high surfaces. Cats, along with camels and giraffes, walk by moving both their left legs, then both their right legs. This helps them walk silently and quickly.

How to Draw a
CAT

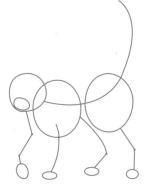

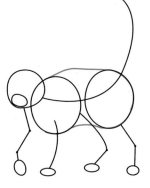

① Start with a simple stick figure of the cat. Use circles for the head and body, ovals for the snout and feet, and lines for the limbs and tail.

② Now, join the two body circles together with a smooth, curved line.

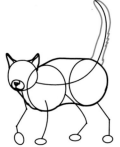

3 Next, use triangles and curved lines to draw the neck, ears, nose, and mouth.

4 In this step, use curved lines to draw the tail.

5 Next, draw the legs.

6 Now, draw the eyes and paws, as shown.

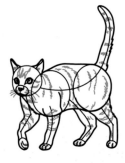

7 Draw the nails and fur on the head, body, and tail using straight and rough lines.

8 Erase the extra lines and the stick figure frame.

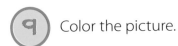

9 Color the picture.

Meet the
DOG

Dogs come in many shapes and sizes. From the tiny Chihuahua to the enormous Irish wolfhound, the appearances of dogs can be quite varied. Despite these differences, all dogs share the same origin. Their common ancestry means that all dogs share a number of the same physical features.

Nose

Dogs use their sense of smell to identify things. The bones inside the nose are covered with scent cells. A dog's sense of smell is one million times better than a human's. A dog's nose also helps it control its body temperature.

Eyes

Dogs do not see as well as humans. They have trouble seeing objects if they are too far away. They also see very little color. Dogs have a third eyelid that helps protect, cleanse, and moisten the eye.

900 million

The approximate number of dogs on Earth.

38.4

Percentage of American households that own at least one dog.

Ears
Dogs have a very keen sense of hearing. Each ear has 17 muscles. These muscles can raise, lower, and turn the outer ear flaps. A dog's ears are excellent at knowing where a sound came from.

Tail
A dog often uses its tail to communicate its feelings. A wagging tail usually means a dog is happy, while a tail that is tucked in means it is afraid.

Feet
Dogs have long, slender feet. The heel of each foot is raised and does not touch the ground. This means that dogs always walk and run on their toes.

Paws
Dogs have tough pads at the bottom of each paw that absorb shock. Claws grip the ground as dogs walk.

How to Draw a
DOG

① Start with a simple stick figure of the dog. Draw circles for the head and body, ovals for the snout and feet, and lines for the limbs.

② Now, join the two body circles together with a curved line.

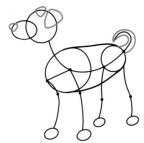

3 Next, draw the nose, ears, and tail, as shown.

4 In this step, use smooth lines to draw the neck.

5 Next, draw the arms and legs, and use curved lines to draw the body.

6 Now, draw the paws.

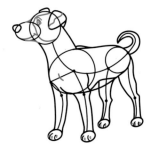

7 Draw the eye, nail, mouth, and snout. Also, add spots on the face and ears.

8 Erase the extra lines and the stick figure frame.

9 Color the picture.

Meet the
FROG

Frog **species** look different from one another. Some frogs are small and thin. Others are large and broad. Although they have different appearances and behaviors, they share many common features.

Skin

A frog absorbs water and oxygen through its skin. Mucus glands help keep the frog's skin moist. Poison glands in its skin help protect the frog from enemies. These poisons are toxic to predators, but they do not often affect humans. A frog's skin is very sensitive to heat and cold, too.

0.4

The length of the gold frog, the world's smallest frog, in inches. (1 centimeter)

12

The length of the West African Goliath frog, the world's largest frog, in inches. (30.5 centimeters)

Legs

Frogs move by jumping. Frogs' legs are strong and powerful. Many frog species can jump very long distances. Frogs have four fingers on their front limbs and five on their back limbs. Frogs that live in water often have webbing between their toes. Most frogs are great swimmers. They use their back legs to push themselves through the water. Their front limbs stay at their sides while they swim.

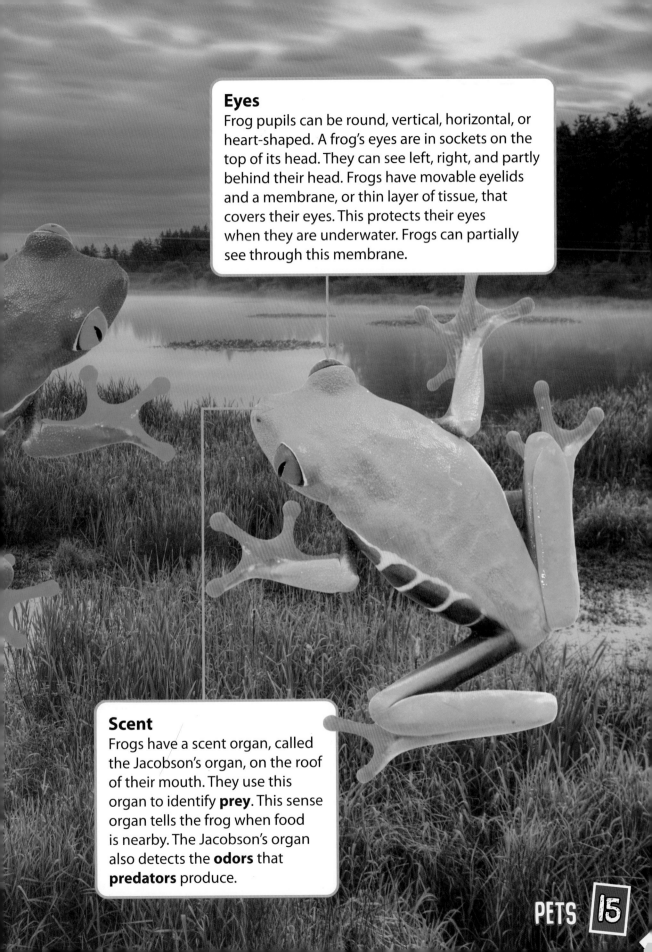

Eyes
Frog pupils can be round, vertical, horizontal, or heart-shaped. A frog's eyes are in sockets on the top of its head. They can see left, right, and partly behind their head. Frogs have movable eyelids and a membrane, or thin layer of tissue, that covers their eyes. This protects their eyes when they are underwater. Frogs can partially see through this membrane.

Scent
Frogs have a scent organ, called the Jacobson's organ, on the roof of their mouth. They use this organ to identify **prey**. This sense organ tells the frog when food is nearby. The Jacobson's organ also detects the **odors** that **predators** produce.

How to Draw a
FROG

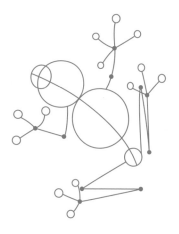

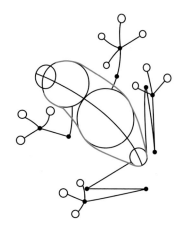

① Start by drawing a simple stick figure of the frog. Use circles for the head, body and feet, an oval for the snout, and lines for the limbs.

② Now, join the head and the two body circles together with a smooth, curved line.

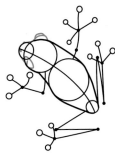

3 Next, draw the eyes and nose using ovals and dots.

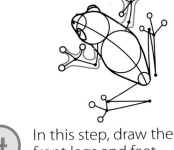

4 In this step, draw the front legs and feet.

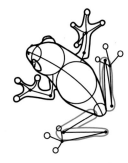

5 Next, draw the hind legs using cylinders.

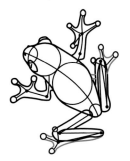

6 Now, draw the hind feet, as shown.

7 Draw small curved lines on the body and legs and rounded spots on the belly.

8 Erase the extra lines and the stick figure frame.

9 Color the picture.

Meet the
GUINEA PIG

Although the various types of guinea pig can look different, they have many of the same features. All guinea pigs are similar sizes and weights. They all have round bodies, short tails, and **fragile** skeletons. They also have thick necks to support their large heads. Guinea pigs have large stomachs that allow them to digest their vegetarian meals easily. They also have short legs so that they never have to crouch down far to pick up food.

20

The approximate number of hours per day that a guinea pig is active.

18.89

The highest jump made by a guinea pig, in inches. (48 centimeters)

Nose
Guinea pigs have a strong sense of smell. They use their little pink noses to sniff out danger.

Mouth
Guinea pigs have 20 teeth. Their teeth are open-rooted, which means that they never stop growing. Guinea pigs use their sharp front teeth to bite and gnaw their food.

YOU CAN DRAW

Eyes

Guinea pigs have large, glossy eyes located on the sides of their head. Guinea pigs can see colors. They are also able to see more images per second than humans. A guinea pig sees 33 images per second, while a human sees an average of 20 images per second.

Ears

Guinea pigs have a good sense of hearing. They are able to hear high-pitched sounds much better than humans. Most guinea pigs are able to recognize other guinea pigs by the sounds they make.

Feet

Guinea pigs have three toes on their back feet and four toes on their front feet. Each foot has sharp claws and leathery soles, or pads, that cover the bottom. These pads help protect the animal's fragile toe bones.

Whiskers

The whiskers on a guinea pig's face are quite long, like a cat's whiskers. Guinea pigs use their whiskers to find objects in the dark.

How to Draw a
GUINEA PIG

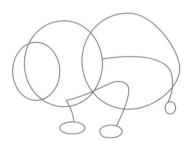

(1) Start with a simple stick figure of the guinea pig. Use circles for the head and body, ovals for the feet, and lines for the limbs.

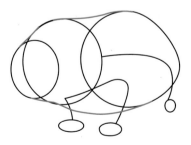

(2) Now, join the circles together with a smooth, curved line.

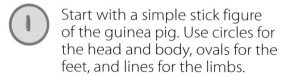

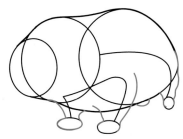

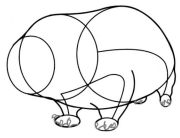

3 Next, draw the legs using curved lines.

4 In this step, draw the feet and nails, as shown.

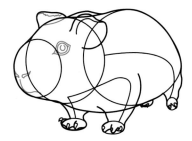

5 Next, draw the ears, as shown.

6 Now, draw the eyes, nose, and mouth, as shown. Also, draw curved lines on the ears.

7 Draw the whiskers and fur.

8 Erase the extra lines and the stick figure frame.

9 Color the picture.

Meet the
SPIDER

With their hard **exoskeleton** and quick movements, spiders have much in common with ants and beetles. However, spiders are not insects. There are several differences between spiders and insects. Insects have six legs and three main body parts. Spiders have eight legs and two main body parts.

Eyes
Most spiders have eight eyes—two large ones and six smaller ones. Most spiders do not see very well.

Fangs
A spider uses its fangs to poison its prey with venom. Using its fangs, the spider injects prey with digestive juices. Most spiders' fangs point toward one another.

Spinnerets

A spider's **silk** comes out of its spinnerets. Spiders spin different kinds of silk for different purposes.

Abdomen

A spider breathes through slits in its abdomen. Its lungs are called book lungs because they look like the pages of a book. Book lungs are not very efficient. A spider cannot run far before it must stop to catch its breath.

Exoskeleton

Spiders have an exoskeleton. This tough shell protects the soft body inside.

Legs

All spiders have eight legs. Spiders taste and smell with their legs.

How to Draw a
SPIDER

1. Start with a simple stick figure of a spider. Draw circles for the head and body and lines for the legs and arms.

2. Use a curved line to join the body circles together.

3 Now, add detail to the body using curved lines.

4 In this step, draw curved rectangular shapes for the legs, as shown.

5 Next, join the rectangular shapes together to form complete legs.

6 Now, add some hair to the head and body.

7 Draw more hair on the head, body, and legs.

8 Erase the extra lines and the stick figure frame.

9 Color the picture.

Meet the
TURTLE

Turtles provide a fascinating link to the past. Ones living today have many of the same traits as turtles from millions of years ago. Turtles are most recognized for the sturdy and beautiful shells that they carry on their back.

Hearing
Unlike humans, turtles do not have ears. Instead, their eardrums are found under the skin or scales, just behind their cheeks. Turtles are able to hear low, deep sounds. Vibrations are also passed through the legs or shell to the ear.

Eyes
Turtles can spot food and dangerous predators from a far distance because they have excellent eyesight.

9 The length, in feet, of the biggest turtle ever to be measured. (3 meters)

60
The average number of bones that make up a turtle shell.

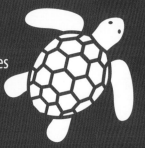

Nose
Turtles have a good sense of smell. This enables them to locate and select their food. A turtle may or may not like certain foods, depending on the smell. Water turtles can smell underwater.

Shell
The **carapace** is joined to the **plastron** by bony bridges. The surface of the shell is made of **keratin**. Different sections on the shell are called scutes. A turtle cannot detach from its shell.

Tail
Most turtles have short tails. Male turtles have longer, thicker, and more pointed tails than female turtles. This is one way to tell males apart from females.

Legs
Land turtles have strong legs to support their heavy shells. Water turtles have long claws and webbed feet. Land turtles have shorter, separate toes that are better suited to land activities, such as digging.

How to Draw a
TURTLE

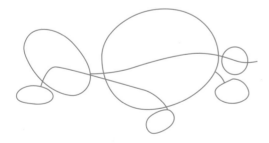

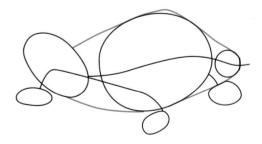

① Start with a simple stick figure of the turtle. Draw a circle for the body, ovals for the head and feet, and lines for the limbs.

② Now, join the head and the two body circles together using a curved line.

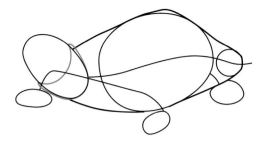
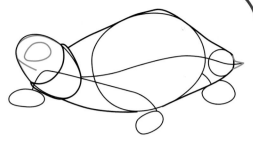

3 Next, draw a curved line on the head, as shown.

4 In this step, draw the mouth and eye in the upper half of the head. Also, draw the tail using a triangle.

5 Add details to the eye, and draw the shell, legs, and feet.

6 Now, draw the spots on the shell.

7 Draw scales on the head and belly, as shown.

8 Erase the extra lines and the figure frame.

9 Color the picture.

Quiz Yourself on
PETS

01 How fast can a domestic cat run?

02 What type of cells cover the bones inside a dog's nose?

03 Where is a frog's Jacobson's organ located?

04 How many images per second can a guinea pig see?

05 What kind of lungs do spiders have?

06 What is one way to tell whether a turtle is male or female?

07 How many muscles does a dog's ear have?

08 What do guinea pigs use their whiskers for?

09 What body parts does a spider use to taste and smell things?

10 Where are a turtle's eardrums located?

ANSWER
01 About 30 miles (48 km) per hour
02 Scent cells **03** On the roof of its mouth
04 33 images per second **05** Book lungs
06 The length of its tail **07** 17 **08** To find
objects in the dark **09** Legs **10** Under the skin
or scales, just behind their cheeks

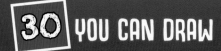

KEY WORDS

carapace: the part of a turtle's shell that is on the back

exoskeleton: the hard outer shell of a spider

fragile: easily broken

habitats: small enclosures where some pets live

independently: one at a time

keratin: a hard substance that forms hair and nails

odors: bad smells

plastron: the section of a turtle's shell that is under the belly

predators: animals that hunt and eat other animals for food

prey: animals that are hunted for food

pupils: the black part of the eyes; regulates how much light enters the eye

retractable claws: claws that can be pulled back into the paw when not in use

silk: a thin, strong material

species: a group of similar animals that can mate together

INDEX

Get the best of both worlds.

AV2 bridges the gap between print and digital.

The expandable resources toolbar enables quick access to content including **videos**, **audio**, **activities**, **weblinks**, **slideshows**, **quizzes**, and **key words**.

Animated videos make static images come alive.

Resource icons on each page help readers to further **explore key concepts**.

Published by AV2
350 5th Avenue, 59th Floor
New York, NY 10118
Website: www.av2books.com

Library of Congress Cataloging-in-Publication Data
Names: McGill, Jordan.
Title: You can draw pets / Jordan McGill.
Description: New York, NY : AV2, [2021] | Includes index. | Audience: Ages
   10-12 | Audience: Grades 4-6
Identifiers: LCCN 2019050477 (print) | LCCN 2019050478 (ebook) | ISBN 9781791119959 (library binding) | ISBN 9781791119966
   (paperback) | ISBN 9781791119973 | ISBN 9781791119980
Subjects: LCSH: Animals in art--Juvenile literature. | Drawing--Technique--Juvenile literature.
Classification: LCC NC783.8.P48 P48 2021 (print) | LCC NC783.8.P48 (ebook) | DDC 743.6--dc23
LC record available at https://lccn.loc.gov/2019050477
LC ebook record available at https://lccn.loc.gov/2019050478

Printed in Guangzhou, China
1 2 3 4 5 6 7 8 9 0 24 23 22 21 20

042020
101319

Project Coordinator: Heather Kissock
Designer: Terry Paulhus